LIVE WITHIN YOUR MEANS

BUDGET
Planner Organizer

INSPIRA
JOURNALS, PLANNERS & NOTEBOOKS

This *Budget Planner* belongs to

NAME: ______________________________

YEAR: ______________________________

Monthly Budget Plan ______________________

BUDGET GOAL: ________________ MONTH: ________________

INCOME			
DATE	DESCRIPTION	AMOUNT	AFTER TAX

FIXED EXPENSES		
DATE	DESCRIPTION	AMOUNT

OTHER EXPENSES		
DATE	DESCRIPTION	AMOUNT

TOTAL	BUDGETED	ACTUAL	DIFFERENCE
EXPENSES			
INCOME			
SAVINGS			

Expense Tracker

DATE	DESCRIPTION	CATEGORY	AMOUNT
TOTAL EXPENSES			

Monthly Budget Plan ____________________

BUDGET GOAL: ____________________ MONTH: ____________________

INCOME			
DATE	DESCRIPTION	AMOUNT	AFTER TAX

FIXED EXPENSES		
DATE	DESCRIPTION	AMOUNT

OTHER EXPENSES		
DATE	DESCRIPTION	AMOUNT

TOTAL	BUDGETED	ACTUAL	DIFFERENCE
EXPENSES			
INCOME			
SAVINGS			

Expense Tracker

DATE	DESCRIPTION	CATEGORY	AMOUNT
TOTAL EXPENSES			

Monthly Budget Plan ______________________

BUDGET GOAL: ________________ MONTH: ________________

INCOME			
DATE	DESCRIPTION	AMOUNT	AFTER TAX

FIXED EXPENSES		
DATE	DESCRIPTION	AMOUNT

OTHER EXPENSES		
DATE	DESCRIPTION	AMOUNT

TOTAL	BUDGETED	ACTUAL	DIFFERENCE
EXPENSES			
INCOME			
SAVINGS			

Expense Tracker

DATE	DESCRIPTION	CATEGORY	AMOUNT
TOTAL EXPENSES			

Monthly Budget Plan ____________________

BUDGET GOAL: ________________ MONTH: ________________

INCOME			
DATE	DESCRIPTION	AMOUNT	AFTER TAX

FIXED EXPENSES		
DATE	DESCRIPTION	AMOUNT

OTHER EXPENSES		
DATE	DESCRIPTION	AMOUNT

TOTAL	BUDGETED	ACTUAL	DIFFERENCE
EXPENSES			
INCOME			
SAVINGS			

Expense Tracker

DATE	DESCRIPTION	CATEGORY	AMOUNT
TOTAL EXPENSES			

Monthly Budget Plan ____________________

BUDGET GOAL: ____________________ MONTH: ____________________

INCOME			
DATE	DESCRIPTION	AMOUNT	AFTER TAX

FIXED EXPENSES		
DATE	DESCRIPTION	AMOUNT

OTHER EXPENSES		
DATE	DESCRIPTION	AMOUNT

TOTAL	BUDGETED	ACTUAL	DIFFERENCE
EXPENSES			
INCOME			
SAVINGS			

Expense Tracker

DATE	DESCRIPTION	CATEGORY	AMOUNT
TOTAL EXPENSES			

Monthly Budget Plan ________________

BUDGET GOAL: ________________ MONTH: ________________

INCOME			
DATE	DESCRIPTION	AMOUNT	AFTER TAX

FIXED EXPENSES		
DATE	DESCRIPTION	AMOUNT

OTHER EXPENSES		
DATE	DESCRIPTION	AMOUNT

TOTAL	BUDGETED	ACTUAL	DIFFERENCE
EXPENSES			
INCOME			
SAVINGS			

Expense Tracker

DATE	DESCRIPTION	CATEGORY	AMOUNT
TOTAL EXPENSES			

Monthly Budget Plan ____________________

BUDGET GOAL: ____________________ MONTH: ____________________

INCOME			
DATE	DESCRIPTION	AMOUNT	AFTER TAX

FIXED EXPENSES		
DATE	DESCRIPTION	AMOUNT

OTHER EXPENSES		
DATE	DESCRIPTION	AMOUNT

TOTAL	BUDGETED	ACTUAL	DIFFERENCE
EXPENSES			
INCOME			
SAVINGS			

Expense Tracker

DATE	DESCRIPTION	CATEGORY	AMOUNT
TOTAL EXPENSES			

Monthly Budget Plan ________________

BUDGET GOAL: ________________ MONTH: ________________

INCOME			
DATE	DESCRIPTION	AMOUNT	AFTER TAX

FIXED EXPENSES		
DATE	DESCRIPTION	AMOUNT

OTHER EXPENSES		
DATE	DESCRIPTION	AMOUNT

TOTAL	BUDGETED	ACTUAL	DIFFERENCE
EXPENSES			
INCOME			
SAVINGS			

Expense Tracker

DATE	DESCRIPTION	CATEGORY	AMOUNT
TOTAL EXPENSES			

Monthly Budget Plan ____________________

BUDGET GOAL: ____________________ MONTH: ____________________

INCOME			
DATE	DESCRIPTION	AMOUNT	AFTER TAX

FIXED EXPENSES		
DATE	DESCRIPTION	AMOUNT

OTHER EXPENSES		
DATE	DESCRIPTION	AMOUNT

TOTAL	BUDGETED	ACTUAL	DIFFERENCE
EXPENSES			
INCOME			
SAVINGS			

Expense Tracker

DATE	DESCRIPTION	CATEGORY	AMOUNT
TOTAL EXPENSES			

Monthly Budget Plan

BUDGET GOAL: ____________________ MONTH: ____________________

INCOME			
DATE	DESCRIPTION	AMOUNT	AFTER TAX

FIXED EXPENSES		
DATE	DESCRIPTION	AMOUNT

OTHER EXPENSES		
DATE	DESCRIPTION	AMOUNT

TOTAL	BUDGETED	ACTUAL	DIFFERENCE
EXPENSES			
INCOME			
SAVINGS			

Expense Tracker

DATE	DESCRIPTION	CATEGORY	AMOUNT
TOTAL EXPENSES			

Monthly Budget Plan ______________________

BUDGET GOAL: ____________________ MONTH: ____________________

INCOME			
DATE	DESCRIPTION	AMOUNT	AFTER TAX

FIXED EXPENSES		
DATE	DESCRIPTION	AMOUNT

OTHER EXPENSES		
DATE	DESCRIPTION	AMOUNT

TOTAL	BUDGETED	ACTUAL	DIFFERENCE
EXPENSES			
INCOME			
SAVINGS			

Expense Tracker

DATE	DESCRIPTION	CATEGORY	AMOUNT
TOTAL EXPENSES			

Monthly Budget Plan ____________________

BUDGET GOAL: ____________________ MONTH: ____________________

INCOME			
DATE	DESCRIPTION	AMOUNT	AFTER TAX

FIXED EXPENSES		
DATE	DESCRIPTION	AMOUNT

OTHER EXPENSES		
DATE	DESCRIPTION	AMOUNT

TOTAL	BUDGETED	ACTUAL	DIFFERENCE
EXPENSES			
INCOME			
SAVINGS			

Expense Tracker

DATE	DESCRIPTION	CATEGORY	AMOUNT
TOTAL EXPENSES			

Monthly Budget Plan ______________________

BUDGET GOAL: ____________________ MONTH: ____________________

INCOME			
DATE	DESCRIPTION	AMOUNT	AFTER TAX

FIXED EXPENSES		
DATE	DESCRIPTION	AMOUNT

OTHER EXPENSES		
DATE	DESCRIPTION	AMOUNT

TOTAL	BUDGETED	ACTUAL	DIFFERENCE
EXPENSES			
INCOME			
SAVINGS			

Expense Tracker

DATE	DESCRIPTION	CATEGORY	AMOUNT
TOTAL EXPENSES			

Savings Tracker

DATE	DEPOSIT	BALANCE

DATE	DEPOSIT	BALANCE

> A budget is telling your money where to go instead of wondering where it went.
> ~ Dave Ramsey

Monthly Budget Plan ____________________

BUDGET GOAL: ____________________ MONTH: ____________________

INCOME			
DATE	DESCRIPTION	AMOUNT	AFTER TAX

FIXED EXPENSES		
DATE	DESCRIPTION	AMOUNT

OTHER EXPENSES		
DATE	DESCRIPTION	AMOUNT

TOTAL	BUDGETED	ACTUAL	DIFFERENCE
EXPENSES			
INCOME			
SAVINGS			

Expense Tracker

DATE	DESCRIPTION	CATEGORY	AMOUNT
TOTAL EXPENSES			

Monthly Budget Plan

BUDGET GOAL: ____________________ MONTH: ____________________

INCOME			
DATE	DESCRIPTION	AMOUNT	AFTER TAX

FIXED EXPENSES		
DATE	DESCRIPTION	AMOUNT

OTHER EXPENSES		
DATE	DESCRIPTION	AMOUNT

TOTAL	BUDGETED	ACTUAL	DIFFERENCE
EXPENSES			
INCOME			
SAVINGS			

Expense Tracker

DATE	DESCRIPTION	CATEGORY	AMOUNT
TOTAL EXPENSES			

Monthly Budget Plan ____________

BUDGET GOAL: ____________ MONTH: ____________

INCOME			
DATE	DESCRIPTION	AMOUNT	AFTER TAX

FIXED EXPENSES		
DATE	DESCRIPTION	AMOUNT

OTHER EXPENSES		
DATE	DESCRIPTION	AMOUNT

TOTAL	BUDGETED	ACTUAL	DIFFERENCE
EXPENSES			
INCOME			
SAVINGS			

Expense Tracker

DATE	DESCRIPTION	CATEGORY	AMOUNT
TOTAL EXPENSES			

Monthly Budget Plan ____________________

BUDGET GOAL: ____________________ MONTH: ____________________

INCOME			
DATE	DESCRIPTION	AMOUNT	AFTER TAX

FIXED EXPENSES		
DATE	DESCRIPTION	AMOUNT

OTHER EXPENSES		
DATE	DESCRIPTION	AMOUNT

TOTAL	BUDGETED	ACTUAL	DIFFERENCE
EXPENSES			
INCOME			
SAVINGS			

Expense Tracker

DATE	DESCRIPTION	CATEGORY	AMOUNT
TOTAL EXPENSES			

Monthly Budget Plan ____________________

BUDGET GOAL: ____________________ MONTH: ____________________

INCOME			
DATE	DESCRIPTION	AMOUNT	AFTER TAX

FIXED EXPENSES		
DATE	DESCRIPTION	AMOUNT

OTHER EXPENSES		
DATE	DESCRIPTION	AMOUNT

TOTAL	BUDGETED	ACTUAL	DIFFERENCE
EXPENSES			
INCOME			
SAVINGS			

Expense Tracker

DATE	DESCRIPTION	CATEGORY	AMOUNT
TOTAL EXPENSES			

Monthly Budget Plan ____________________

BUDGET GOAL: ____________________ MONTH: ____________________

INCOME			
DATE	DESCRIPTION	AMOUNT	AFTER TAX

FIXED EXPENSES		
DATE	DESCRIPTION	AMOUNT

OTHER EXPENSES		
DATE	DESCRIPTION	AMOUNT

TOTAL	BUDGETED	ACTUAL	DIFFERENCE
EXPENSES			
INCOME			
SAVINGS			

Expense Tracker

DATE	DESCRIPTION	CATEGORY	AMOUNT
TOTAL EXPENSES			

Monthly Budget Plan

BUDGET GOAL: ____________________ MONTH: ____________________

INCOME			
DATE	DESCRIPTION	AMOUNT	AFTER TAX

FIXED EXPENSES		
DATE	DESCRIPTION	AMOUNT

OTHER EXPENSES		
DATE	DESCRIPTION	AMOUNT

TOTAL	BUDGETED	ACTUAL	DIFFERENCE
EXPENSES			
INCOME			
SAVINGS			

Expense Tracker

DATE	DESCRIPTION	CATEGORY	AMOUNT
TOTAL EXPENSES			

Monthly Budget Plan ____________________

BUDGET GOAL: ____________________ MONTH: ____________________

INCOME			
DATE	DESCRIPTION	AMOUNT	AFTER TAX

FIXED EXPENSES		
DATE	DESCRIPTION	AMOUNT

OTHER EXPENSES		
DATE	DESCRIPTION	AMOUNT

TOTAL	BUDGETED	ACTUAL	DIFFERENCE
EXPENSES			
INCOME			
SAVINGS			

Expense Tracker

DATE	DESCRIPTION	CATEGORY	AMOUNT
TOTAL EXPENSES			

Monthly Budget Plan ____________________

BUDGET GOAL: ____________________ MONTH: ____________________

INCOME			
DATE	DESCRIPTION	AMOUNT	AFTER TAX

FIXED EXPENSES		
DATE	DESCRIPTION	AMOUNT

OTHER EXPENSES		
DATE	DESCRIPTION	AMOUNT

TOTAL	BUDGETED	ACTUAL	DIFFERENCE
EXPENSES			
INCOME			
SAVINGS			

Expense Tracker

DATE	DESCRIPTION	CATEGORY	AMOUNT
TOTAL EXPENSES			

Monthly Budget Plan

BUDGET GOAL: ____________________ MONTH: ____________________

INCOME			
DATE	DESCRIPTION	AMOUNT	AFTER TAX

FIXED EXPENSES		
DATE	DESCRIPTION	AMOUNT

OTHER EXPENSES		
DATE	DESCRIPTION	AMOUNT

TOTAL	BUDGETED	ACTUAL	DIFFERENCE
EXPENSES			
INCOME			
SAVINGS			

Expense Tracker

DATE	DESCRIPTION	CATEGORY	AMOUNT
TOTAL EXPENSES			

Monthly Budget Plan ______________________

BUDGET GOAL: ________________ MONTH: ________________

INCOME			
DATE	DESCRIPTION	AMOUNT	AFTER TAX

FIXED EXPENSES		
DATE	DESCRIPTION	AMOUNT

OTHER EXPENSES		
DATE	DESCRIPTION	AMOUNT

TOTAL	BUDGETED	ACTUAL	DIFFERENCE
EXPENSES			
INCOME			
SAVINGS			

Expense Tracker

DATE	DESCRIPTION	CATEGORY	AMOUNT
TOTAL EXPENSES			

Monthly Budget Plan ____________

BUDGET GOAL: ____________ MONTH: ____________

INCOME			
DATE	DESCRIPTION	AMOUNT	AFTER TAX

FIXED EXPENSES		
DATE	DESCRIPTION	AMOUNT

OTHER EXPENSES		
DATE	DESCRIPTION	AMOUNT

TOTAL	BUDGETED	ACTUAL	DIFFERENCE
EXPENSES			
INCOME			
SAVINGS			

Expense Tracker

DATE	DESCRIPTION	CATEGORY	AMOUNT
TOTAL EXPENSES			

Monthly Budget Plan

BUDGET GOAL: ______________ MONTH: ______________

INCOME			
DATE	DESCRIPTION	AMOUNT	AFTER TAX

FIXED EXPENSES		
DATE	DESCRIPTION	AMOUNT

OTHER EXPENSES		
DATE	DESCRIPTION	AMOUNT

TOTAL	BUDGETED	ACTUAL	DIFFERENCE
EXPENSES			
INCOME			
SAVINGS			

Expense Tracker

DATE	DESCRIPTION	CATEGORY	AMOUNT
TOTAL EXPENSES			

Debt Tracker

ACCOUNT:	
MINIMUM:	DUE DATE:
CREDIT LIMIT:	INTEREST RATE:

BALANCE	PAYMENT	DATE	NEW BALANCE

Budgets are blueprints and priorities.
~ Kevin McCarthy

Monthly Budget Plan ______________________

BUDGET GOAL: ________________ MONTH: ________________

INCOME			
DATE	DESCRIPTION	AMOUNT	AFTER TAX

FIXED EXPENSES		
DATE	DESCRIPTION	AMOUNT

OTHER EXPENSES		
DATE	DESCRIPTION	AMOUNT

TOTAL	BUDGETED	ACTUAL	DIFFERENCE
EXPENSES			
INCOME			
SAVINGS			

Expense Tracker

DATE	DESCRIPTION	CATEGORY	AMOUNT
TOTAL EXPENSES			

Monthly Budget Plan ______________________

BUDGET GOAL: ________________ MONTH: ________________

INCOME			
DATE	DESCRIPTION	AMOUNT	AFTER TAX

FIXED EXPENSES		
DATE	DESCRIPTION	AMOUNT

OTHER EXPENSES		
DATE	DESCRIPTION	AMOUNT

TOTAL	BUDGETED	ACTUAL	DIFFERENCE
EXPENSES			
INCOME			
SAVINGS			

Expense Tracker

DATE	DESCRIPTION	CATEGORY	AMOUNT
TOTAL EXPENSES			

Monthly Budget Plan ____________________

BUDGET GOAL: ____________________ MONTH: ____________________

INCOME			
DATE	DESCRIPTION	AMOUNT	AFTER TAX

FIXED EXPENSES		
DATE	DESCRIPTION	AMOUNT

OTHER EXPENSES		
DATE	DESCRIPTION	AMOUNT

TOTAL	BUDGETED	ACTUAL	DIFFERENCE
EXPENSES			
INCOME			
SAVINGS			

Expense Tracker

DATE	DESCRIPTION	CATEGORY	AMOUNT
TOTAL EXPENSES			

Monthly Budget Plan ____________________

BUDGET GOAL: ____________________ MONTH: ____________________

INCOME			
DATE	DESCRIPTION	AMOUNT	AFTER TAX

FIXED EXPENSES		
DATE	DESCRIPTION	AMOUNT

OTHER EXPENSES		
DATE	DESCRIPTION	AMOUNT

TOTAL	BUDGETED	ACTUAL	DIFFERENCE
EXPENSES			
INCOME			
SAVINGS			

Expense Tracker

DATE	DESCRIPTION	CATEGORY	AMOUNT
TOTAL EXPENSES			

Monthly Budget Plan ______________________

BUDGET GOAL: ________________ MONTH: ________________

INCOME			
DATE	DESCRIPTION	AMOUNT	AFTER TAX

FIXED EXPENSES		
DATE	DESCRIPTION	AMOUNT

OTHER EXPENSES		
DATE	DESCRIPTION	AMOUNT

TOTAL	BUDGETED	ACTUAL	DIFFERENCE
EXPENSES			
INCOME			
SAVINGS			

Expense Tracker

DATE	DESCRIPTION	CATEGORY	AMOUNT
TOTAL EXPENSES			

Monthly Budget Plan ____________________

BUDGET GOAL: ________________ MONTH: ________________

INCOME			
DATE	DESCRIPTION	AMOUNT	AFTER TAX

FIXED EXPENSES		
DATE	DESCRIPTION	AMOUNT

OTHER EXPENSES		
DATE	DESCRIPTION	AMOUNT

TOTAL	BUDGETED	ACTUAL	DIFFERENCE
EXPENSES			
INCOME			
SAVINGS			

Expense Tracker

DATE	DESCRIPTION	CATEGORY	AMOUNT
TOTAL EXPENSES			

Monthly Budget Plan ____________________

BUDGET GOAL: ________________ MONTH: ________________

INCOME			
DATE	DESCRIPTION	AMOUNT	AFTER TAX

FIXED EXPENSES		
DATE	DESCRIPTION	AMOUNT

OTHER EXPENSES		
DATE	DESCRIPTION	AMOUNT

TOTAL	BUDGETED	ACTUAL	DIFFERENCE
EXPENSES			
INCOME			
SAVINGS			

Expense Tracker

DATE	DESCRIPTION	CATEGORY	AMOUNT
TOTAL EXPENSES			

Monthly Budget Plan

BUDGET GOAL: ____________________ MONTH: ____________________

INCOME			
DATE	DESCRIPTION	AMOUNT	AFTER TAX

FIXED EXPENSES		
DATE	DESCRIPTION	AMOUNT

OTHER EXPENSES		
DATE	DESCRIPTION	AMOUNT

TOTAL	BUDGETED	ACTUAL	DIFFERENCE
EXPENSES			
INCOME			
SAVINGS			

Expense Tracker

DATE	DESCRIPTION	CATEGORY	AMOUNT
TOTAL EXPENSES			

Monthly Budget Plan

BUDGET GOAL: ________________ MONTH: ________________

INCOME			
DATE	DESCRIPTION	AMOUNT	AFTER TAX

FIXED EXPENSES		
DATE	DESCRIPTION	AMOUNT

OTHER EXPENSES		
DATE	DESCRIPTION	AMOUNT

TOTAL	BUDGETED	ACTUAL	DIFFERENCE
EXPENSES			
INCOME			
SAVINGS			

Expense Tracker

DATE	DESCRIPTION	CATEGORY	AMOUNT
TOTAL EXPENSES			

Monthly Budget Plan ____________________

BUDGET GOAL: ____________________ MONTH: ____________________

INCOME			
DATE	DESCRIPTION	AMOUNT	AFTER TAX

FIXED EXPENSES		
DATE	DESCRIPTION	AMOUNT

OTHER EXPENSES		
DATE	DESCRIPTION	AMOUNT

TOTAL	BUDGETED	ACTUAL	DIFFERENCE
EXPENSES			
INCOME			
SAVINGS			

Expense Tracker

DATE	DESCRIPTION	CATEGORY	AMOUNT
TOTAL EXPENSES			

Monthly Budget Plan ______________________

BUDGET GOAL: ________________ MONTH: ________________

INCOME			
DATE	DESCRIPTION	AMOUNT	AFTER TAX

FIXED EXPENSES		
DATE	DESCRIPTION	AMOUNT

OTHER EXPENSES		
DATE	DESCRIPTION	AMOUNT

TOTAL	BUDGETED	ACTUAL	DIFFERENCE
EXPENSES			
INCOME			
SAVINGS			

Expense Tracker

DATE	DESCRIPTION	CATEGORY	AMOUNT
TOTAL EXPENSES			

Monthly Budget Plan

BUDGET GOAL: ____________________ MONTH: ____________________

INCOME			
DATE	DESCRIPTION	AMOUNT	AFTER TAX

FIXED EXPENSES		
DATE	DESCRIPTION	AMOUNT

OTHER EXPENSES		
DATE	DESCRIPTION	AMOUNT

TOTAL	BUDGETED	ACTUAL	DIFFERENCE
EXPENSES			
INCOME			
SAVINGS			

Expense Tracker

DATE	DESCRIPTION	CATEGORY	AMOUNT
TOTAL EXPENSES			

Monthly Budget Plan

BUDGET GOAL: ________________ MONTH: ________________

INCOME			
DATE	DESCRIPTION	AMOUNT	AFTER TAX

FIXED EXPENSES		
DATE	DESCRIPTION	AMOUNT

OTHER EXPENSES		
DATE	DESCRIPTION	AMOUNT

TOTAL	BUDGETED	ACTUAL	DIFFERENCE
EXPENSES			
INCOME			
SAVINGS			

Expense Tracker

DATE	DESCRIPTION	CATEGORY	AMOUNT
TOTAL EXPENSES			

Savings Tracker

DATE	DEPOSIT	BALANCE

DATE	DEPOSIT	BALANCE

The budget is not just a collection
of numbers, but an expression of our
values and aspirations.
~ Jacob Lew

Monthly Budget Plan

BUDGET GOAL: ____________ MONTH: ____________

INCOME			
DATE	DESCRIPTION	AMOUNT	AFTER TAX

FIXED EXPENSES		
DATE	DESCRIPTION	AMOUNT

OTHER EXPENSES		
DATE	DESCRIPTION	AMOUNT

TOTAL	BUDGETED	ACTUAL	DIFFERENCE
EXPENSES			
INCOME			
SAVINGS			

Expense Tracker

DATE	DESCRIPTION	CATEGORY	AMOUNT
TOTAL EXPENSES			

Monthly Budget Plan ____________

BUDGET GOAL: ____________ MONTH: ____________

INCOME			
DATE	DESCRIPTION	AMOUNT	AFTER TAX

FIXED EXPENSES		
DATE	DESCRIPTION	AMOUNT

OTHER EXPENSES		
DATE	DESCRIPTION	AMOUNT

TOTAL	BUDGETED	ACTUAL	DIFFERENCE
EXPENSES			
INCOME			
SAVINGS			

Expense Tracker

DATE	DESCRIPTION	CATEGORY	AMOUNT
TOTAL EXPENSES			

Monthly Budget Plan ______________________

BUDGET GOAL: ____________________ MONTH: ____________________

INCOME			
DATE	DESCRIPTION	AMOUNT	AFTER TAX

FIXED EXPENSES		
DATE	DESCRIPTION	AMOUNT

OTHER EXPENSES		
DATE	DESCRIPTION	AMOUNT

TOTAL	BUDGETED	ACTUAL	DIFFERENCE
EXPENSES			
INCOME			
SAVINGS			

Expense Tracker

DATE	DESCRIPTION	CATEGORY	AMOUNT
TOTAL EXPENSES			

Monthly Budget Plan ____________________

BUDGET GOAL: ____________________ MONTH: ____________________

INCOME			
DATE	DESCRIPTION	AMOUNT	AFTER TAX

FIXED EXPENSES		
DATE	DESCRIPTION	AMOUNT

OTHER EXPENSES		
DATE	DESCRIPTION	AMOUNT

TOTAL	BUDGETED	ACTUAL	DIFFERENCE
EXPENSES			
INCOME			
SAVINGS			

Expense Tracker

DATE	DESCRIPTION	CATEGORY	AMOUNT
TOTAL EXPENSES			

Monthly Budget Plan

BUDGET GOAL: ________________ MONTH: ________________

INCOME			
DATE	DESCRIPTION	AMOUNT	AFTER TAX

FIXED EXPENSES		
DATE	DESCRIPTION	AMOUNT

OTHER EXPENSES		
DATE	DESCRIPTION	AMOUNT

TOTAL	BUDGETED	ACTUAL	DIFFERENCE
EXPENSES			
INCOME			
SAVINGS			

Expense Tracker

DATE	DESCRIPTION	CATEGORY	AMOUNT
TOTAL EXPENSES			

Monthly Budget Plan ______________________

BUDGET GOAL: ____________________ MONTH: ____________________

INCOME			
DATE	DESCRIPTION	AMOUNT	AFTER TAX

FIXED EXPENSES		
DATE	DESCRIPTION	AMOUNT

OTHER EXPENSES		
DATE	DESCRIPTION	AMOUNT

TOTAL	BUDGETED	ACTUAL	DIFFERENCE
EXPENSES			
INCOME			
SAVINGS			

Expense Tracker

DATE	DESCRIPTION	CATEGORY	AMOUNT
TOTAL EXPENSES			

Monthly Budget Plan ____________

BUDGET GOAL: ____________ MONTH: ____________

INCOME			
DATE	DESCRIPTION	AMOUNT	AFTER TAX

FIXED EXPENSES		
DATE	DESCRIPTION	AMOUNT

OTHER EXPENSES		
DATE	DESCRIPTION	AMOUNT

TOTAL	BUDGETED	ACTUAL	DIFFERENCE
EXPENSES			
INCOME			
SAVINGS			

Expense Tracker

DATE	DESCRIPTION	CATEGORY	AMOUNT
TOTAL EXPENSES			

Monthly Budget Plan ______________________

BUDGET GOAL: ________________ MONTH: ________________

INCOME			
DATE	DESCRIPTION	AMOUNT	AFTER TAX

FIXED EXPENSES		
DATE	DESCRIPTION	AMOUNT

OTHER EXPENSES		
DATE	DESCRIPTION	AMOUNT

TOTAL	BUDGETED	ACTUAL	DIFFERENCE
EXPENSES			
INCOME			
SAVINGS			

Expense Tracker

DATE	DESCRIPTION	CATEGORY	AMOUNT
TOTAL EXPENSES			

Monthly Budget Plan ____________________

BUDGET GOAL: ____________________ MONTH: ____________________

INCOME			
DATE	DESCRIPTION	AMOUNT	AFTER TAX

FIXED EXPENSES		
DATE	DESCRIPTION	AMOUNT

OTHER EXPENSES		
DATE	DESCRIPTION	AMOUNT

TOTAL	BUDGETED	ACTUAL	DIFFERENCE
EXPENSES			
INCOME			
SAVINGS			

Expense Tracker

DATE	DESCRIPTION	CATEGORY	AMOUNT
TOTAL EXPENSES			

Monthly Budget Plan ____________________

BUDGET GOAL: ____________________ MONTH: ____________________

INCOME			
DATE	DESCRIPTION	AMOUNT	AFTER TAX

FIXED EXPENSES		
DATE	DESCRIPTION	AMOUNT

OTHER EXPENSES		
DATE	DESCRIPTION	AMOUNT

TOTAL	BUDGETED	ACTUAL	DIFFERENCE
EXPENSES			
INCOME			
SAVINGS			

Expense Tracker

DATE	DESCRIPTION	CATEGORY	AMOUNT
TOTAL EXPENSES			

Monthly Budget Plan ______________________

BUDGET GOAL: ________________ MONTH: ________________

INCOME			
DATE	DESCRIPTION	AMOUNT	AFTER TAX

FIXED EXPENSES		
DATE	DESCRIPTION	AMOUNT

OTHER EXPENSES		
DATE	DESCRIPTION	AMOUNT

TOTAL	BUDGETED	ACTUAL	DIFFERENCE
EXPENSES			
INCOME			
SAVINGS			

Expense Tracker

DATE	DESCRIPTION	CATEGORY	AMOUNT
TOTAL EXPENSES			

Monthly Budget Plan ____________________

BUDGET GOAL: ____________________ MONTH: ____________________

INCOME			
DATE	DESCRIPTION	AMOUNT	AFTER TAX

FIXED EXPENSES		
DATE	DESCRIPTION	AMOUNT

OTHER EXPENSES		
DATE	DESCRIPTION	AMOUNT

TOTAL	BUDGETED	ACTUAL	DIFFERENCE
EXPENSES			
INCOME			
SAVINGS			

Expense Tracker

DATE	DESCRIPTION	CATEGORY	AMOUNT
TOTAL EXPENSES			

Monthly Budget Plan ______________________

BUDGET GOAL: ________________ MONTH: ________________

INCOME			
DATE	DESCRIPTION	AMOUNT	AFTER TAX

FIXED EXPENSES		
DATE	DESCRIPTION	AMOUNT

OTHER EXPENSES		
DATE	DESCRIPTION	AMOUNT

TOTAL	BUDGETED	ACTUAL	DIFFERENCE
EXPENSES			
INCOME			
SAVINGS			

Expense Tracker

DATE	DESCRIPTION	CATEGORY	AMOUNT
TOTAL EXPENSES			

Debt Tracker

ACCOUNT:	
MINIMUM:	DUE DATE:
CREDIT LIMIT:	INTEREST RATE:

BALANCE	PAYMENT	DATE	NEW BALANCE

Manage your spending by creating and sticking to a budget.
~ Alexa Von Tobel

Monthly Budget Plan ____________________

BUDGET GOAL: ____________________ MONTH: ____________________

INCOME			
DATE	DESCRIPTION	AMOUNT	AFTER TAX

FIXED EXPENSES		
DATE	DESCRIPTION	AMOUNT

OTHER EXPENSES		
DATE	DESCRIPTION	AMOUNT

TOTAL	BUDGETED	ACTUAL	DIFFERENCE
EXPENSES			
INCOME			
SAVINGS			

Expense Tracker

DATE	DESCRIPTION	CATEGORY	AMOUNT
TOTAL EXPENSES			

Monthly Budget Plan ______________________

BUDGET GOAL: ________________ MONTH: ________________

INCOME			
DATE	DESCRIPTION	AMOUNT	AFTER TAX

FIXED EXPENSES		
DATE	DESCRIPTION	AMOUNT

OTHER EXPENSES		
DATE	DESCRIPTION	AMOUNT

TOTAL	BUDGETED	ACTUAL	DIFFERENCE
EXPENSES			
INCOME			
SAVINGS			

Expense Tracker

DATE	DESCRIPTION	CATEGORY	AMOUNT
TOTAL EXPENSES			

Monthly Budget Plan ____________________

BUDGET GOAL: ____________________ MONTH: ____________________

INCOME			
DATE	DESCRIPTION	AMOUNT	AFTER TAX

FIXED EXPENSES		
DATE	DESCRIPTION	AMOUNT

OTHER EXPENSES		
DATE	DESCRIPTION	AMOUNT

TOTAL	BUDGETED	ACTUAL	DIFFERENCE
EXPENSES			
INCOME			
SAVINGS			

Expense Tracker

DATE	DESCRIPTION	CATEGORY	AMOUNT
TOTAL EXPENSES			

Monthly Budget Plan ______________________

BUDGET GOAL: __________________ MONTH: __________________

INCOME			
DATE	DESCRIPTION	AMOUNT	AFTER TAX

FIXED EXPENSES		
DATE	DESCRIPTION	AMOUNT

OTHER EXPENSES		
DATE	DESCRIPTION	AMOUNT

TOTAL	BUDGETED	ACTUAL	DIFFERENCE
EXPENSES			
INCOME			
SAVINGS			

Expense Tracker

DATE	DESCRIPTION	CATEGORY	AMOUNT
TOTAL EXPENSES			

Monthly Budget Plan ______________________

BUDGET GOAL: __________________ MONTH: __________________

INCOME			
DATE	DESCRIPTION	AMOUNT	AFTER TAX

FIXED EXPENSES		
DATE	DESCRIPTION	AMOUNT

OTHER EXPENSES		
DATE	DESCRIPTION	AMOUNT

TOTAL	BUDGETED	ACTUAL	DIFFERENCE
EXPENSES			
INCOME			
SAVINGS			

Expense Tracker

DATE	DESCRIPTION	CATEGORY	AMOUNT
TOTAL EXPENSES			

Monthly Budget Plan

BUDGET GOAL: ____________________ MONTH: ____________________

INCOME			
DATE	DESCRIPTION	AMOUNT	AFTER TAX

FIXED EXPENSES		
DATE	DESCRIPTION	AMOUNT

OTHER EXPENSES		
DATE	DESCRIPTION	AMOUNT

TOTAL	BUDGETED	ACTUAL	DIFFERENCE
EXPENSES			
INCOME			
SAVINGS			

Expense Tracker

DATE	DESCRIPTION	CATEGORY	AMOUNT
TOTAL EXPENSES			

Monthly Budget Plan ____________________

BUDGET GOAL: ____________________ MONTH: ____________________

INCOME			
DATE	DESCRIPTION	AMOUNT	AFTER TAX

FIXED EXPENSES		
DATE	DESCRIPTION	AMOUNT

OTHER EXPENSES		
DATE	DESCRIPTION	AMOUNT

TOTAL	BUDGETED	ACTUAL	DIFFERENCE
EXPENSES			
INCOME			
SAVINGS			

Expense Tracker

DATE	DESCRIPTION	CATEGORY	AMOUNT
TOTAL EXPENSES			

Monthly Budget Plan

BUDGET GOAL: ____________________ MONTH: ____________________

INCOME			
DATE	DESCRIPTION	AMOUNT	AFTER TAX

FIXED EXPENSES		
DATE	DESCRIPTION	AMOUNT

OTHER EXPENSES		
DATE	DESCRIPTION	AMOUNT

TOTAL	BUDGETED	ACTUAL	DIFFERENCE
EXPENSES			
INCOME			
SAVINGS			

Expense Tracker

DATE	DESCRIPTION	CATEGORY	AMOUNT
TOTAL EXPENSES			

Monthly Budget Plan ______________________

BUDGET GOAL: ________________ MONTH: ________________

INCOME			
DATE	DESCRIPTION	AMOUNT	AFTER TAX

FIXED EXPENSES		
DATE	DESCRIPTION	AMOUNT

OTHER EXPENSES		
DATE	DESCRIPTION	AMOUNT

TOTAL	BUDGETED	ACTUAL	DIFFERENCE
EXPENSES			
INCOME			
SAVINGS			

Expense Tracker

DATE	DESCRIPTION	CATEGORY	AMOUNT
TOTAL EXPENSES			

Monthly Budget Plan ______________________________

BUDGET GOAL: ____________________ MONTH: ____________________

INCOME			
DATE	DESCRIPTION	AMOUNT	AFTER TAX

FIXED EXPENSES		
DATE	DESCRIPTION	AMOUNT

OTHER EXPENSES		
DATE	DESCRIPTION	AMOUNT

TOTAL	BUDGETED	ACTUAL	DIFFERENCE
EXPENSES			
INCOME			
SAVINGS			

Expense Tracker

DATE	DESCRIPTION	CATEGORY	AMOUNT
TOTAL EXPENSES			

Monthly Budget Plan ______________________

BUDGET GOAL: __________________ MONTH: __________________

INCOME			
DATE	DESCRIPTION	AMOUNT	AFTER TAX

FIXED EXPENSES		
DATE	DESCRIPTION	AMOUNT

OTHER EXPENSES		
DATE	DESCRIPTION	AMOUNT

TOTAL	BUDGETED	ACTUAL	DIFFERENCE
EXPENSES			
INCOME			
SAVINGS			

Expense Tracker

DATE	DESCRIPTION	CATEGORY	AMOUNT
TOTAL EXPENSES			

Monthly Budget Plan ______________________

BUDGET GOAL: __________________ MONTH: __________________

INCOME			
DATE	DESCRIPTION	AMOUNT	AFTER TAX

FIXED EXPENSES		
DATE	DESCRIPTION	AMOUNT

OTHER EXPENSES		
DATE	DESCRIPTION	AMOUNT

TOTAL	BUDGETED	ACTUAL	DIFFERENCE
EXPENSES			
INCOME			
SAVINGS			

Expense Tracker

DATE	DESCRIPTION	CATEGORY	AMOUNT
TOTAL EXPENSES			

Monthly Budget Plan ____________________

BUDGET GOAL: ____________________ MONTH: ____________________

INCOME			
DATE	DESCRIPTION	AMOUNT	AFTER TAX

FIXED EXPENSES		
DATE	DESCRIPTION	AMOUNT

OTHER EXPENSES		
DATE	DESCRIPTION	AMOUNT

TOTAL	BUDGETED	ACTUAL	DIFFERENCE
EXPENSES			
INCOME			
SAVINGS			

Expense Tracker

DATE	DESCRIPTION	CATEGORY	AMOUNT
TOTAL EXPENSES			

Savings Tracker

DATE	DEPOSIT	BALANCE

DATE	DEPOSIT	BALANCE

Budgets are nothing if not statements of priorities.
~ Jeff Merkley

Monthly Budget Plan

BUDGET GOAL: ________________ MONTH: ________________

INCOME			
DATE	DESCRIPTION	AMOUNT	AFTER TAX

FIXED EXPENSES		
DATE	DESCRIPTION	AMOUNT

OTHER EXPENSES		
DATE	DESCRIPTION	AMOUNT

TOTAL	BUDGETED	ACTUAL	DIFFERENCE
EXPENSES			
INCOME			
SAVINGS			

Expense Tracker

DATE	DESCRIPTION	CATEGORY	AMOUNT
TOTAL EXPENSES			

Monthly Budget Plan ____________

BUDGET GOAL: ____________ MONTH: ____________

INCOME			
DATE	DESCRIPTION	AMOUNT	AFTER TAX

FIXED EXPENSES		
DATE	DESCRIPTION	AMOUNT

OTHER EXPENSES		
DATE	DESCRIPTION	AMOUNT

TOTAL	BUDGETED	ACTUAL	DIFFERENCE
EXPENSES			
INCOME			
SAVINGS			

Expense Tracker

DATE	DESCRIPTION	CATEGORY	AMOUNT
TOTAL EXPENSES			

Monthly Budget Plan ______________________

BUDGET GOAL: ____________________ MONTH: ____________________

INCOME			
DATE	DESCRIPTION	AMOUNT	AFTER TAX

FIXED EXPENSES		
DATE	DESCRIPTION	AMOUNT

OTHER EXPENSES		
DATE	DESCRIPTION	AMOUNT

TOTAL	BUDGETED	ACTUAL	DIFFERENCE
EXPENSES			
INCOME			
SAVINGS			

Expense Tracker

DATE	DESCRIPTION	CATEGORY	AMOUNT
TOTAL EXPENSES			

Monthly Budget Plan ____________________

BUDGET GOAL: ____________________ MONTH: ____________________

INCOME			
DATE	DESCRIPTION	AMOUNT	AFTER TAX

FIXED EXPENSES		
DATE	DESCRIPTION	AMOUNT

OTHER EXPENSES		
DATE	DESCRIPTION	AMOUNT

TOTAL	BUDGETED	ACTUAL	DIFFERENCE
EXPENSES			
INCOME			
SAVINGS			

Expense Tracker

DATE	DESCRIPTION	CATEGORY	AMOUNT
TOTAL EXPENSES			

Monthly Budget Plan ____________________

BUDGET GOAL: ____________________ MONTH: ____________________

INCOME			
DATE	DESCRIPTION	AMOUNT	AFTER TAX

FIXED EXPENSES		
DATE	DESCRIPTION	AMOUNT

OTHER EXPENSES		
DATE	DESCRIPTION	AMOUNT

TOTAL	BUDGETED	ACTUAL	DIFFERENCE
EXPENSES			
INCOME			
SAVINGS			

Expense Tracker

DATE	DESCRIPTION	CATEGORY	AMOUNT
TOTAL EXPENSES			

Monthly Budget Plan

BUDGET GOAL: ____________________ MONTH: ____________________

INCOME			
DATE	DESCRIPTION	AMOUNT	AFTER TAX

FIXED EXPENSES		
DATE	DESCRIPTION	AMOUNT

OTHER EXPENSES		
DATE	DESCRIPTION	AMOUNT

TOTAL	BUDGETED	ACTUAL	DIFFERENCE
EXPENSES			
INCOME			
SAVINGS			

Expense Tracker

DATE	DESCRIPTION	CATEGORY	AMOUNT
TOTAL EXPENSES			

Monthly Budget Plan ____________________

BUDGET GOAL: ____________________ MONTH: ____________________

INCOME			
DATE	DESCRIPTION	AMOUNT	AFTER TAX

FIXED EXPENSES		
DATE	DESCRIPTION	AMOUNT

OTHER EXPENSES		
DATE	DESCRIPTION	AMOUNT

TOTAL	BUDGETED	ACTUAL	DIFFERENCE
EXPENSES			
INCOME			
SAVINGS			

Expense Tracker

DATE	DESCRIPTION	CATEGORY	AMOUNT
TOTAL EXPENSES			

Monthly Budget Plan ______________________

BUDGET GOAL: ________________ MONTH: ________________

INCOME			
DATE	DESCRIPTION	AMOUNT	AFTER TAX

FIXED EXPENSES		
DATE	DESCRIPTION	AMOUNT

OTHER EXPENSES		
DATE	DESCRIPTION	AMOUNT

TOTAL	BUDGETED	ACTUAL	DIFFERENCE
EXPENSES			
INCOME			
SAVINGS			

Expense Tracker

DATE	DESCRIPTION	CATEGORY	AMOUNT
TOTAL EXPENSES			

Monthly Budget Plan ____________________

BUDGET GOAL: ____________________ MONTH: ____________________

INCOME			
DATE	DESCRIPTION	AMOUNT	AFTER TAX

FIXED EXPENSES		
DATE	DESCRIPTION	AMOUNT

OTHER EXPENSES		
DATE	DESCRIPTION	AMOUNT

TOTAL	BUDGETED	ACTUAL	DIFFERENCE
EXPENSES			
INCOME			
SAVINGS			

Expense Tracker

DATE	DESCRIPTION	CATEGORY	AMOUNT
TOTAL EXPENSES			

Monthly Budget Plan ________________

BUDGET GOAL: ________________ MONTH: ________________

INCOME			
DATE	DESCRIPTION	AMOUNT	AFTER TAX

FIXED EXPENSES		
DATE	DESCRIPTION	AMOUNT

OTHER EXPENSES		
DATE	DESCRIPTION	AMOUNT

TOTAL	BUDGETED	ACTUAL	DIFFERENCE
EXPENSES			
INCOME			
SAVINGS			

Expense Tracker

DATE	DESCRIPTION	CATEGORY	AMOUNT
TOTAL EXPENSES			

Monthly Budget Plan ______________________

BUDGET GOAL: ________________ MONTH: ________________

INCOME			
DATE	DESCRIPTION	AMOUNT	AFTER TAX

FIXED EXPENSES		
DATE	DESCRIPTION	AMOUNT

OTHER EXPENSES		
DATE	DESCRIPTION	AMOUNT

TOTAL	BUDGETED	ACTUAL	DIFFERENCE
EXPENSES			
INCOME			
SAVINGS			

Expense Tracker

DATE	DESCRIPTION	CATEGORY	AMOUNT
TOTAL EXPENSES			

Monthly Budget Plan ____________________

BUDGET GOAL: __________________ MONTH: __________________

INCOME			
DATE	DESCRIPTION	AMOUNT	AFTER TAX

FIXED EXPENSES		
DATE	DESCRIPTION	AMOUNT

OTHER EXPENSES		
DATE	DESCRIPTION	AMOUNT

TOTAL	BUDGETED	ACTUAL	DIFFERENCE
EXPENSES			
INCOME			
SAVINGS			

Expense Tracker

DATE	DESCRIPTION	CATEGORY	AMOUNT
TOTAL EXPENSES			

Monthly Budget Plan ______________________

BUDGET GOAL: ________________ MONTH: ________________

INCOME			
DATE	DESCRIPTION	AMOUNT	AFTER TAX

FIXED EXPENSES		
DATE	DESCRIPTION	AMOUNT

OTHER EXPENSES		
DATE	DESCRIPTION	AMOUNT

TOTAL	BUDGETED	ACTUAL	DIFFERENCE
EXPENSES			
INCOME			
SAVINGS			

Expense Tracker

DATE	DESCRIPTION	CATEGORY	AMOUNT
TOTAL EXPENSES			

Debt Tracker

ACCOUNT:	
MINIMUM:	DUE DATE:
CREDIT LIMIT:	INTEREST RATE:

BALANCE	PAYMENT	DATE	NEW BALANCE

The safe way to double your money is to fold it over once and put it in your pocket.
~ Frank Hubbard
THE UNITED STATES OF AMERICA
ONE

Monthly Budget Plan

BUDGET GOAL: ________________ MONTH: ________________

INCOME			
DATE	DESCRIPTION	AMOUNT	AFTER TAX

FIXED EXPENSES		
DATE	DESCRIPTION	AMOUNT

OTHER EXPENSES		
DATE	DESCRIPTION	AMOUNT

TOTAL	BUDGETED	ACTUAL	DIFFERENCE
EXPENSES			
INCOME			
SAVINGS			

Expense Tracker

DATE	DESCRIPTION	CATEGORY	AMOUNT
TOTAL EXPENSES			

Monthly Budget Plan

BUDGET GOAL: ____________________ MONTH: ____________________

INCOME			
DATE	DESCRIPTION	AMOUNT	AFTER TAX

FIXED EXPENSES		
DATE	DESCRIPTION	AMOUNT

OTHER EXPENSES		
DATE	DESCRIPTION	AMOUNT

TOTAL	BUDGETED	ACTUAL	DIFFERENCE
EXPENSES			
INCOME			
SAVINGS			

Expense Tracker

DATE	DESCRIPTION	CATEGORY	AMOUNT
TOTAL EXPENSES			

Monthly Budget Plan ____________________

BUDGET GOAL: ____________________ MONTH: ____________________

INCOME			
DATE	DESCRIPTION	AMOUNT	AFTER TAX

FIXED EXPENSES		
DATE	DESCRIPTION	AMOUNT

OTHER EXPENSES		
DATE	DESCRIPTION	AMOUNT

TOTAL	BUDGETED	ACTUAL	DIFFERENCE
EXPENSES			
INCOME			
SAVINGS			

Expense Tracker

DATE	DESCRIPTION	CATEGORY	AMOUNT
TOTAL EXPENSES			

Monthly Budget Plan ____________

BUDGET GOAL: ____________ MONTH: ____________

INCOME			
DATE	DESCRIPTION	AMOUNT	AFTER TAX

FIXED EXPENSES		
DATE	DESCRIPTION	AMOUNT

OTHER EXPENSES		
DATE	DESCRIPTION	AMOUNT

TOTAL	BUDGETED	ACTUAL	DIFFERENCE
EXPENSES			
INCOME			
SAVINGS			

Expense Tracker

DATE	DESCRIPTION	CATEGORY	AMOUNT
TOTAL EXPENSES			

Monthly Budget Plan ____________

BUDGET GOAL: ______________ MONTH: ______________

INCOME			
DATE	DESCRIPTION	AMOUNT	AFTER TAX

FIXED EXPENSES		
DATE	DESCRIPTION	AMOUNT

OTHER EXPENSES		
DATE	DESCRIPTION	AMOUNT

TOTAL	BUDGETED	ACTUAL	DIFFERENCE
EXPENSES			
INCOME			
SAVINGS			

Expense Tracker

DATE	DESCRIPTION	CATEGORY	AMOUNT
TOTAL EXPENSES			

Monthly Budget Plan ____________

BUDGET GOAL: ____________ MONTH: ____________

INCOME			
DATE	DESCRIPTION	AMOUNT	AFTER TAX

FIXED EXPENSES		
DATE	DESCRIPTION	AMOUNT

OTHER EXPENSES		
DATE	DESCRIPTION	AMOUNT

TOTAL	BUDGETED	ACTUAL	DIFFERENCE
EXPENSES			
INCOME			
SAVINGS			

Expense Tracker

DATE	DESCRIPTION	CATEGORY	AMOUNT
TOTAL EXPENSES			

Monthly Budget Plan ____________________

BUDGET GOAL: ____________________ MONTH: ____________________

INCOME			
DATE	DESCRIPTION	AMOUNT	AFTER TAX

FIXED EXPENSES		
DATE	DESCRIPTION	AMOUNT

OTHER EXPENSES		
DATE	DESCRIPTION	AMOUNT

TOTAL	BUDGETED	ACTUAL	DIFFERENCE
EXPENSES			
INCOME			
SAVINGS			

Expense Tracker

DATE	DESCRIPTION	CATEGORY	AMOUNT
TOTAL EXPENSES			

Monthly Budget Plan ____________

BUDGET GOAL: ____________ MONTH: ____________

INCOME			
DATE	DESCRIPTION	AMOUNT	AFTER TAX

FIXED EXPENSES		
DATE	DESCRIPTION	AMOUNT

OTHER EXPENSES		
DATE	DESCRIPTION	AMOUNT

TOTAL	BUDGETED	ACTUAL	DIFFERENCE
EXPENSES			
INCOME			
SAVINGS			

Expense Tracker

DATE	DESCRIPTION	CATEGORY	AMOUNT
TOTAL EXPENSES			

Monthly Budget Plan ________________

BUDGET GOAL: ________________ MONTH: ________________

INCOME			
DATE	DESCRIPTION	AMOUNT	AFTER TAX

FIXED EXPENSES		
DATE	DESCRIPTION	AMOUNT

OTHER EXPENSES		
DATE	DESCRIPTION	AMOUNT

TOTAL	BUDGETED	ACTUAL	DIFFERENCE
EXPENSES			
INCOME			
SAVINGS			

Expense Tracker

DATE	DESCRIPTION	CATEGORY	AMOUNT
TOTAL EXPENSES			

Monthly Budget Plan ______________________

BUDGET GOAL: ______________ MONTH: ______________

INCOME			
DATE	DESCRIPTION	AMOUNT	AFTER TAX

FIXED EXPENSES		
DATE	DESCRIPTION	AMOUNT

OTHER EXPENSES		
DATE	DESCRIPTION	AMOUNT

TOTAL	BUDGETED	ACTUAL	DIFFERENCE
EXPENSES			
INCOME			
SAVINGS			

Expense Tracker

DATE	DESCRIPTION	CATEGORY	AMOUNT
TOTAL EXPENSES			

Monthly Budget Plan

BUDGET GOAL: ________________ MONTH: ________________

INCOME			
DATE	DESCRIPTION	AMOUNT	AFTER TAX

FIXED EXPENSES		
DATE	DESCRIPTION	AMOUNT

OTHER EXPENSES		
DATE	DESCRIPTION	AMOUNT

TOTAL	BUDGETED	ACTUAL	DIFFERENCE
EXPENSES			
INCOME			
SAVINGS			

Expense Tracker

DATE	DESCRIPTION	CATEGORY	AMOUNT
TOTAL EXPENSES			

Monthly Budget Plan ______________________

BUDGET GOAL: ________________ MONTH: ________________

INCOME			
DATE	DESCRIPTION	AMOUNT	AFTER TAX

FIXED EXPENSES		
DATE	DESCRIPTION	AMOUNT

OTHER EXPENSES		
DATE	DESCRIPTION	AMOUNT

TOTAL	BUDGETED	ACTUAL	DIFFERENCE
EXPENSES			
INCOME			
SAVINGS			

Expense Tracker

DATE	DESCRIPTION	CATEGORY	AMOUNT
TOTAL EXPENSES			

Monthly Budget Plan ____________________

BUDGET GOAL: ____________________ MONTH: ____________________

INCOME			
DATE	DESCRIPTION	AMOUNT	AFTER TAX

FIXED EXPENSES		
DATE	DESCRIPTION	AMOUNT

OTHER EXPENSES		
DATE	DESCRIPTION	AMOUNT

TOTAL	BUDGETED	ACTUAL	DIFFERENCE
EXPENSES			
INCOME			
SAVINGS			

Expense Tracker

DATE	DESCRIPTION	CATEGORY	AMOUNT
TOTAL EXPENSES			

Savings Tracker

DATE	DEPOSIT	BALANCE

DATE	DEPOSIT	BALANCE

Money is a terrible master but
an excellent servant.
~ P.T. Barnum

Made in United States
North Haven, CT
04 October 2022

24964768R00111